AUSTRALIAN BICENTENNIAL
COLLECTION

1788-1988

Heads of a Plan for effectually disposing of Convicts, and rendering their Transportation reciprocally beneficial both to themselves and to the State, by the Establishment of a Colony in New South Wales, a Country which by the fertility and salubrity of the Climate, connected with the remoteness of its situation (from whence it is hardly possible for persons to return without permission) seems peculiarly adapted to answer the views of Government with respect to the providing a remedy for the evils likely to result by the late alarming and numerous encrease of Felons in

AUSTRALIAN BICENTENNIAL COLLECTION
Book 1 *The First Australians*
Book 2 *Navigators and Shipwrecks*
Book 3 *Botany Bay*

Illustrations:
Cover: Joseph Banks, by Sir Joshua Reynolds
This page: *Heads of a Plan*, 18 August 1786
Title page: *Banksia serrata*

BOTANY BAY
Australia's heritage in stamps

● Australia Post

Compiled by Christine Hogarth, Australia Post Stamps & Philatelic Branch

Designed by Keryn Christos, Australia Post Graphic Design Studio.

© Australia Post 1986

Typesetters: Typographical Services, Melbourne
Colour separators: Enticott Polygraph, Melbourne
Printer: The Griffin Press, Adelaide

ISBN 0 642 099138

William Pitt, British Prime Minister, addressing the
House of Commons

Contents

New Holland: Cook's Voyage

INTRODUCTION

For 50,000 years, Aboriginal society flourished in the isolation of the island continent now known as Australia. Then less than 400 years ago, in the first decade of the seventeenth century, European navigators began returning home with charts showing sections of a new coastline, sometimes after literally bumping into the western shore of this land whilst en route for the East Indies [Indonesia]. By the end of the seventeenth century, Dutch and English navigators had mapped the continent's northern, western and southern shores from western Cape York Peninsula to the Great Australian Bight, as well as about half of the Tasmanian coast. The continent became known as New Holland.

Its eastern coast remained elusive however, and the apparent barrenness of the shores already discovered dampened the enthusiasm of the European merchant powers–there seemed little prospect for trade. It was not until the late eighteenth century that there was a resurgence of interest and then, between 1770 and 1786, discoveries were made and decisions taken which would change forever the fate of the land and its inhabitants.

It is the events of those sixteen years with which this third stamp heritage book is concerned. The series began in 1984 with *The First Australians,* a tribute to our Aboriginal heritage, whilst the exploits and trials of the early European navigators were traced in the second stamp heritage book, *Navigators and Shipwrecks* (1985). Future stamp heritage books will trace the voyage of the First Fleet and the early years of settlement in New South Wales.

By the mid-eighteenth century, England and France had overtaken the Netherlands and Spain as the major European trading powers, and competition between the two rival countries was fierce. Ever alert for fresh avenues of trade and hoping to find sites suitable for strategic bases, each nation began renewed exploration of the Pacific during the 1760s. English navigators John Byron, Samuel Wallis and Philip Carteret all completed circumnavigations of the world at this time.

In June 1768 the great French explorer, Louis de Bougainville, came within a hair's breadth of discovering New Holland's eastern coast, but he turned away at the sight of the treacherous reefs guarding the northern Queensland shoreline. The privilege of this dramatic discovery thus awaited the arrival, less than two years later, of Lieutenant James Cook of the Royal Navy.

JAMES COOK

Born in 1728 in Yorkshire, England, the son of a labourer, James Cook rose from his humble beginnings to become possibly the greatest navigator in maritime history. His intelligence was recognised early and he received a somewhat better education than would normally have been his lot. In 1746 at the age of eighteen Cook became apprenticed to a coal-shipping firm at Whitby–his career at sea had begun. He learnt his seacraft plying up and down England's eastern coast, transporting coal to the metropolis of London.

By 1755 Cook had proved himself worthy of the captaincy of one of the firm's ships. In June of that year, however, when England and France were on the verge of war, he opted to join the Royal Navy as an able seaman. His experience and abilities earned him the position of Master's Mate within a month aboard his first Navy ship.

Two years later Cook obtained his Master's ticket. Although not a commissioned officer, the Master aboard each Navy vessel was responsible for navigation, surveying, recording, supplies and general management, subject to the Captain's instructions. Between 1758 and 1762 Cook served as Master aboard various Navy ships in the war against the French in North America, becoming skilled in mapping waterways and harbours.

He returned to England in 1762 but went back to North America several times over the next five years to survey and chart the Newfoundland coast. In 1768 he was preparing to depart for a further season's work there, when he was instead ordered to a new command.

THE VOYAGE OF THE *ENDEAVOUR*

The Royal Society, Britain's leading scientific organisation in the late eighteenth century, was keen to send observers to the southern Pacific Ocean to observe the transit of the planet Venus in front of the sun in 1769. Precise observations of this event would determine the earth's distance from the sun, greatly advancing the sciences of astronomy and navigation. King George III agreed to provide the necessary funds and supply a Navy vessel and crew–the King and his government had an additional task in mind for this expedition.

In April 1768 the Admiralty purchased a shallow-draught ship of the type known as a 'cat', the very same type of vessel upon which Cook had trained. Originally called *Earl of Pembroke,* the vessel was renamed *Endeavour.* Cook was promoted to Lieutenant and appointed commander of the expedition on the basis of his skills in navigation, mapping and observation, and his reputation as an excellent Master. He was then forty years of age, a seaman of twenty-two years experience.

It took several months for the *Endeavour* to be refitted, for the crew to be found and supplies to be gathered. The vessel was only some thirty metres long and nine metres wide, yet into this small ship were to be crammed a crew of eighty-five men and a scientific complement of eleven, together with several animals, including two dogs and a goat, and supplies to last for three years. Little wonder that Dr Samuel Johnson, the eighteenth century literary figure remarked:

No man will be a sailor who has contrivance enough to get himself into a jail; for being in a ship is like being in a jail, with the chance of being drowned.

The scientific party aboard was originally to consist only of an astronomer and his servant, with Cook himself acting as the second observer of the transit. However just a few weeks before the *Endeavour* was due to sail, permission was granted for Joseph Banks, a Fellow of the Royal Society and a passionate botanist, to bring aboard a party of naturalists at his own expense, 'for the Advancement of useful knowledge'. Cook had to find room for Banks' party of nine, even giving up his great cabin, the only suitable space for the group to work.

Accompanying Banks were Dr Daniel Solander, a Swedish naturalist working for the British Museum; Sydney Parkinson, a botanical artist; Alexander Buchan, a painter of landscapes and portraits; Herman Sporing, a Swedish watchmaker and draughtsman with training in surgery, who acted as Banks' secretary; and four servants.

Australia's coastline before Cook's voyage

The Admiralty's plan of the Endeavour

James Cook

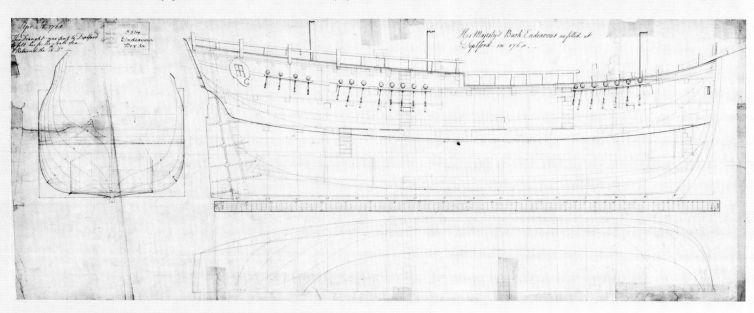

Cook's sailing instructions were finalised in late July. Firstly, he was to sail to Tahiti where the transit of Venus would be observed. Then he was to proceed forthwith to the south in search of 'a Continent or Land of great extent' until reaching the latitude of 40° South, where he was to turn westward 'until you discover it, or fall in with the Eastern side of the Land discover'd by Tasman and now called New Zeland.'

If Cook did discover the southern continent, he was instructed to explore the coast, make charts and record all possible observations about its natural history and inhabitants and 'with the Consent of the Natives to take possession of Convenient Situations in the Country in the Name of the King of Great Britain.'

BRITAIN TO NEW ZEALAND

In the last week of August 1768 the *Endeavour* left Plymouth bound for Tahiti, via Madeira, Rio de Janeiro and Cape Horn. The vessel arrived in Matavai Bay, Tahiti, on 13 April 1769 and the transit of Venus was duly observed in June. After a thorough overhaul, the *Endeavour* set sail in August on the second part of its journey.

In his search for the southern continent and New Zealand, Cook had one great advantage over the navigators who had preceded him in these waters. Advances in the science of navigation in the mid-eighteenth century meant that Cook was one of the first seafaring explorers to use reliable methods of determining both latitude and longitude by means of astronomical and mathematical principles. He knew exactly where he was on the globe and could accurately record the location of any lands discovered.

On 6 October 1769 the coast of New Zealand was sighted and Cook spent six months circumnavigating and charting both the south and north islands. Then, in consultation with his crew, he decided to sail westwards in search of the southern continent before turning north for the East Indies and home.

NEW HOLLAND: DISCOVERY

Cook headed for Van Diemen's Land [Tasmania] in the latitude in which it had been reported by Tasman in the 1640s, but a southerly gale drove the *Endeavour* to the north. At 6 a.m. on 19 April 1770 the eastern coast of New Holland was sighted by Europeans probably for the first time. Cook recorded that:

...at 6 saw land extending from NE to West at the distance of 5 or 6 Leagues...The Southern most Point of land we had in sight...I have Named it Points Hicks, because Lieut't Hicks was the first who discover'd this land.

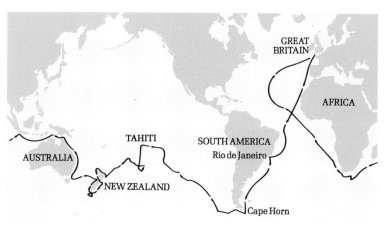

GREAT BRITAIN

AFRICA

TAHITI

SOUTH AMERICA
Rio de Janeiro

AUSTRALIA

NEW ZEALAND

Cape Horn

Sailing north along this new coast, Cook charted and named bays and landmarks and periodically hoisted the British flag, claiming possession of the land in the name of the King. It seems unlikely, however, that he was able to obtain 'the Consent of the Natives' to these claims as had been specified in his instructions.

BOTANY BAY

On 28 April, in search of fresh water, the *Endeavour* sailed into a bay 'which appeared to be tolerably well sheltered from all winds.' A landing party went ashore in an attempt to make friendly contact with a group of Aborigines but 'they all made off except two men who seemed resolved to oppose our landing.' The Aboriginal men threw spears and stones at the crew before retreating.

The *Endeavour* remained in this bay for over a week, while Cook and his men explored the hinterland, collected water and wood, and tried to initiate peaceful communication with the local people. Banks and his party meanwhile enthusiastically gathered hundreds of new plants, drawing and recording them in a frenzy of activity. Cook and the naturalists also saw the tracks of strange animals, the nature of which was not to be determined for several more weeks.

Cook originally planned to call the bay 'Stingray's Harbour', but later recorded that:

The great quantity of New Plants etc Mr Banks & Dr Solander collected in this place occasioned my giveing it the name of Botany Bay...

DISASTER

After leaving Botany Bay, Cook sailed northwards past Port Jackson, Newcastle, Moreton Bay, Great Keppel Island and Shoalwater Bay. In early June he navigated the Whitsunday Passage, sailed past Magnetic Island and landed parties on Palm Island and Cape Grafton (see map page 39).

Then, on 10 June disaster threatened–the *Endeavour* was holed when it struck part of the Great Barrier Reef! Many tonnes of goods were thrown overboard to lighten the vessel and everyone aboard took turns to man the pumps. After almost twenty-four hours, it was hauled off the reef. The *Endeavour* sailed slowly towards the mainland, while members of the crew plugged the leak as best they could.

The vessel was beached in the mouth of a river which was also to be named the Endeavour, in northern Queensland, on 16 June. Repairs took seven weeks to complete, giving the naturalists plenty of time to survey the surrounding country and add to their ever-growing collections. It was during this period that they were at last able to examine a kangaroo. On 14 July Banks recorded that:

Our second lieutenant who was a shooting today had the good fortune to kill the animal that had so long been the subject of our speculations. To compare it to any European animal would be impossible as it has not the least resemblance of any one I have seen. Its fore legs are extremely short and of no use to it in walking, its hind again as disproportionaly long; with these it hops 7 or 8 feet at each hop...

Cook's voyage 1768-1771

Parkinson's sketch of a kangaroo

The naturalists discover a kangaroo

Two Aborigines of New South Wales, by Parkinson

The Endeavour beached at the Endeavour River, Queensland

HOMEWARD BOUND

During the first week of August, the *Endeavour* left the river and sailed cautiously northwards. The northernmost point of the continent was reached on 21 August and Cook landed on Possession Island:

...I now once more hoisted English Coulers and in the Name of His Majesty King George the Third took possession of the whole Eastern Coast from the above Latitude [38° South] down to this place by the name of New South Wales, together with all the Bays, Harbours Rivers and Islands situate upon the said coast...

After leaving Possession Island, Cook headed for Batavia [Djakarta] in the East Indies, arriving there on 11 October 1770. The crew had been remarkably free of scurvy and other illnesses despite the length of the journey. At Batavia, however, almost all aboard succumbed to malaria or dysentery, and many died. The *Endeavour* left Batavia for England on 26 December 1770 but twenty-three more men died on the journey, including Mr Green the astronomer, Herman Sporing and Sydney Parkinson. On 12 July 1771 the *Endeavour* finally arrived home, its complement tragically depleted.

RESULTS AND RECOGNITION

This epic voyage of discovery is now remembered as Cook's voyage, but at the time the *Endeavour* returned to England it was Banks who received popular acclaim. Newspapers were full of stories of Banks' exploits and he and Solander were presented to the King. The 'curiosities' brought back by Banks excited a great deal of interest and the distinguished scientist, Linnaeus, even suggested that the new land be called 'Banksia'.

Of Lieutenant Cook, barely a word was reported, despite his having returned with a resource even more valuable to the nation than Banks' unique natural history collection–detailed charts of Tahiti, New Zealand and the long, fertile, eastern coast of New Holland. The latter charts later enabled the British government to establish a penal settlement there. He had taken formal possession of New South Wales for Great Britain and had rediscovered Torres Strait, lost to sight since Torres first sailed through it in 1606. He had also kept at bay the great scourge of shipboard life, scurvy, no mean feat in the late eighteenth century.

Cook quietly and efficiently reported the results of his voyage to the Admiralty and the Royal Society, was presented to the King and promoted to Commander. In August 1771 he wrote to his former employer at Whitby:

...the Voyage has fully Answered the expectation of my Superiors...I however have made no very great Discoveries yet I have exploar'd more of the Great South Sea than all that have gone before me so much that little remains now to be done to have a thorough knowledge of that part of the Globe...

With his reputation as a master navigator now firmly established, Cook undertook two further voyages of exploration. On his second voyage (1772-5), he succeeded in finding and circumnavigating Antarctica. He was promoted to Post-Captain after this voyage and also elected a Fellow of the Royal Society–recognition of his achievements at last.

His third and final voyage (1776-9) was prompted by the search for a North-West Passage to the Far East via North America. After exploring the Pacific coasts of Siberia and North America, Cook sailed to Hawaii where he was killed in a confrontation with the inhabitants on 14 February 1779.

Joseph Banks

Joseph Banks was born in 1743, the only son of a wealthy land-owning family. From an early age, his declared passion was natural history, and in particular, botany. Shortly after inheriting his family's fortune in the early 1760s, he chose to pursue this passion to the full. In 1766 he travelled to Newfoundland and Labrador to collect plants, animals and rocks and was elected a Fellow of the Royal Society in the same year.

When the Royal Society was successful in initiating the expedition to Tahiti, he obtained permission from the Admiralty to join the venture. For Banks, this was like a present-day botanist being given the chance of a trip to another planet, a chance to study new plants in unknown lands.

After his triumphant return from Cook's first voyage, Banks travelled to Scotland, Wales, Holland and Iceland, collecting more and more 'curiosities'. Amongst a host of other activities, including the running of his estates, he controlled the Royal Botanic Gardens in Kew and was a Trustee of the British Museum. In 1778 he also became President of the Royal Society, an office which he held until his death in 1820. He was knighted in 1781.

Although Linnaeus' suggestion of naming the new country 'Banksia' was not adopted, Banks' name was bestowed upon a genus of Australian plants and he made his mark upon Australian history in more ways than one. When the British government was casting about for a suitable place to establish a penal colony, Banks was an advocate for Botany Bay. After the settlement was established at Sydney Cove, he encouraged further investigation of the natural history of the area and became the acknowledged authority on any and all matters relating to New South Wales. His impact on the study of natural history in both Britain and Australia cannot be overestimated.

The 'Banks' stamp features a portrait by Sir Joshua Reynolds, reproduced with the permission of Parham Park, England; a detail from the late nineteenth century 'Captain Cook' stained glass window by John Lamb Lyon at Cranbrook School, Sydney, showing Banks conferring with Dr Solander; and Banks' signature, from a manuscript in the National Library of Australia.

Joseph Banks

Banks conferring with Solander at Botany Bay

Sydney Parkinson

To Sydney Parkinson, as much as to Banks, do we owe the stunning record of Australian botany brought back aboard the *Endeavour*. If Banks' curiosity, enthusiasm and money formed the basis for the venture, it was Parkinson's skill as an artist which brought it to life.

Parkinson was born in Edinburgh about 1745, the younger son of a Quaker brewer. During his teenage years he learnt to draw, and:

...taking a particular delight in drawing flowers, fruit, and other objects of natural history, he became soon so proficient in that style of painting, as to attract the notice of the most celebrated botanists and connoisseurs of that study.

In 1764 or 1765 Parkinson moved to London with his mother and began giving drawing lessons to the daughter of James Lee, nurseryman and botanist. It was Lee who introduced Parkinson to Joseph Banks. Recognising Parkinson's talent, Banks employed him to illustrate specimens from Newfoundland and Labrador and when the expedition to the southern seas was approved, Parkinson was the logical choice to accompany Banks as a specialist artist of natural history.

He quickly developed a special shorthand technique for botanical illustration, drawing an outline sketch of the whole plant but only filling in the detail and colour of one or two flowers, buds, leaves, seeds and stems. A few days after the *Endeavour* left Botany Bay, Banks recorded:

This evening we finishd Drawing the plants got in the last harbour, which had been kept fresh till this time by means of tin chests and wet cloths. In 14 days just, one draughtsman has made 94 sketch drawings, so quick a hand has he acquird by use.

Parkinson intended to produce complete watercolour illustrations from these sketches upon his return to England, but tragically he died aboard ship in late January 1771. His work was later completed by a team of artists employed by Banks.

The 'Parkinson' stamp features a self-portrait, held by the British Museum (Natural History); a detail from an engraving showing Parkinson at work from the frontispiece to his posthumously published journal; and Parkinson's signature.

Parkinson at his desk

Sydney Parkinson

Sydney Parkinson

Banksia serrata
New South Wales Botany Bay J.B.

Banksia serrata
Collected: Botany Bay,
            New South Wales;
            April-May 1770
Sketch: Sydney Parkinson
Watercolour: J. F. Miller, 1773

Banks' Florilegium: Collecting & Recording

Throughout the voyage, Banks and Solander collected specimens of the living things around them at every opportunity and certainly whenever they were able to go ashore. They collected examples of over 1,000 species of animals including 370 species of arthropods, about 500 species of molluscs, fish and other marine animals, and over 100 species of birds. In addition, they gathered over 30,000 individual plant specimens representing about 3,600 species, of which some 1,400 were completely new to science at that time. How they ever managed to store all these in the already overcrowded *Endeavour* is indeed a mystery!

The naturalists maintained their enthusiasm for the duration of the voyage, always having plenty to keep them busy, a boon on such a long journey:

...I wish that our friends in England could by the assistance of some magical spying glass take a peep at our situation: Dr Solander setts at the Cabbin table describing, myself [Banks] at my Bureau Journalizing, between us hangs a large bunch of sea weed, upon the table lays the wood and barnacles; they would see that notwithstanding our different occupations our lips move very often, and without being conjurors might guess that we were talking about what we should see upon the land...

Banks and Solander kept Parkinson and Sporing constantly working too, drawing specimens and recording details of their provenance and habitat. Banks described a typical working day aboard ship:

...seldom was there a storm strong enough to break up our normal study time, which lasted daily from nearly 8 o'clock in the morning till 2 in the afternoon. From 4 or 5, when the cabin has lost the odour of food, we sat till dark by the great table with our draughtsman opposite and showed him in what way to make his drawings, and ourselves made rapid descriptions of all the details of natural history while our specimens were still fresh.

Parkinson's sketch

Watercolour illustration

Hibiscus meraukensis
Cape Grafton New Holland

Hibiscus meraukensis
Collected: Cape Grafton,
                Queensland;
                June 1770
Sketch: Sydney Parkinson
Watercolour: F. P. Nodder, 1778

Banks' Florilegium: Collecting & Recording Continued

For Parkinson in particular, conditions often made it difficult for him to draw:

The flies [in Tahiti]...eat the painters colours off the paper as fast as they can be laid on, and if a fish is to be drawn there is more trouble in keeping them off it than in the drawing itself.

Many expedients have been thought of, none succeed better than a mosquito net which covers table chair painter and drawings, but even that is not sufficient, a fly trap was necessary to set within this to atract the vermin from eating the colours. For that purpose yesterday tarr and molasses was mixt together but did not succeed. The plate smeard with it was left on the outside of the tent to clean: one of the Indians observing this took an opportunity when he thought that no one observd him to take some of this mixture... the gentleman had a large sore upon his backside to which this clammy liniament was applyd but with what success I never took the pains to enquire.

Nevertheless, Parkinson succeeded in drawing hundreds of specimens, including over 400 Australian plants, far exceeding even the demanding expectations of his employer.

Each of the botanical stamps in the *New Holland: Cook's Voyage* set features a retouched detail from Parkinson's original sketch overlaid upon the watercolour illustration of the plant, reproduced with the permission of the British Museum (Natural History).

Watercolour illustration

Parkinson's sketch

Cleaning a Florilegium copperplate (see p 23)

Dillenia alata
Endeavour River New Holland

Dillenia alata
Collected: Endeavour River,
Queensland;
June-August 1770
Sketch: Sydney Parkinson
Watercolour: F. P. Nodder, 1778

Banks' Florilegium: After the Voyage

Banks planned to transform Parkinson's botanical sketches into watercolour illustrations and then to have them engraved and printed to form a *Florilegium*. He gathered together teams of artists to paint the watercolours and engravers to produce the copperplates. By 1785, 743 engraved plates had been prepared from the watercolours (337 of them Australian plants) and Banks had spent 7,000 pounds on the project, a fortune at that time. But there the project stopped. The *Florilegium* was never published during Banks' lifetime but the reasons for this sudden halt are not clear.

It has been suggested that Banks' income had declined providing insufficient funds to continue the work. Alternatively, perhaps he simply lost interest, swamped by the myriad of other activities in which he was involved. He bequeathed the plates to the British Museum and they are now stored in the British Museum (Natural History).

Parkinson's sketch

Watercolour illustration

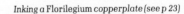

Inking a Florilegium copperplate (see p 23)

Botany store at British Museum (Natural History)

21

Correa reflexa
New South Wales Botany Bay

Correa reflexa
Collected: Botany Bay,
          New South Wales;
          April-May 1770
Sketch: Sydney Parkinson
Watercolour: J. F. Miller, 1775

Banks' Florilegium: Publication

In 1978 the British Museum (Natural History) began a co-operative venture with Alecto Historical Editions to print, in full colour and accurate detail, each of the surviving 738 plates in a limited edition of 110 copies, using printing methods as close as possible to those of the late eighteenth century.

The technique requires that all the colours be printed at the same time, the printer applying the necessary pigments to the leaves, flowers, stems and seeds each time a print is made. It can take up to two months to get the colours right and perfect the impression of just one plate. Constant comparisons with the watercolour illustrations and the original specimens themselves are required to maintain the quality of the prints. Most of the 100 sets for sale are being bought by libraries and museums around the world, including several Australian institutions.

Parkinson's sketch

Watercolour illustration

Alecto's printing press

New South Wales: The Decision To Settle

AMERICAN INDEPENDENCE

In an ironic twist of fate Botany Bay, named by Cook in honour of the beautiful, strange new plants surrounding it, soon became a name symbolising exile, dreaded by the English criminal classes.

The American War of Independence erupted in 1775, four years after Cook returned from his first voyage to the Pacific. For many years the development of the American economy had been hampered by restrictions imposed upon it by dint of its being a British colony. The Americans were tired of paying what they felt to be extravagant taxes while being forced to accept the edicts of a remote and seemingly tyrannical government. They wanted freedom to trade, freedom to govern themselves.

Not until 1783 was peace negotiated and formalised by the Treaty of Versailles. Canada and Nova Scotia remained British, Louisiana was French and Florida Spanish, but America, stretching east from the Mississippi and north from Florida as far as the Great Lakes, was independent.

One of the side effects of both the war and the peace was that America could no longer be used by the British government as a dumping ground for its convicts sentenced to transportation.

TRANSPORTATION

There were four main punishments for crime in eighteenth century Britain—corporal punishment, imprisonment, transportation and death. Corporal punishment was the sentence for such crimes as petty theft and minor assault, while imprisonment was used sparingly because of the cost involved in maintaining the jails, for debtors, frauds and perjurers. Transportation and death were reserved for the most serious offences, as perceived at the time.

Transportation had been used as a method of disposing of prisoners since the early 1600s, but had not become a common punishment until 1717, when Parliament passed an Act laying the basis for regular transportation of convicts to the American colonies for use as cheap labour.

Crimes for which transportation was the punishment included murder and manslaughter, picking pockets, burglary and housebreaking, robbery, embezzlement, poaching and other larcenies, forgery, assault, rape, receiving stolen goods, arson and treason. Between 1760 and 1774, about 70% of all sentences handed down by the courts were for transportation, compared to less than 2% for imprisonment.

About 30,000 convicts were sent to America between 1717 and 1775. When this outlet was cut off, a great strain was placed upon Britain's inadequate prison system. There was insufficient room to house all the extra convicts and insufficient funds to provide more room at short notice.

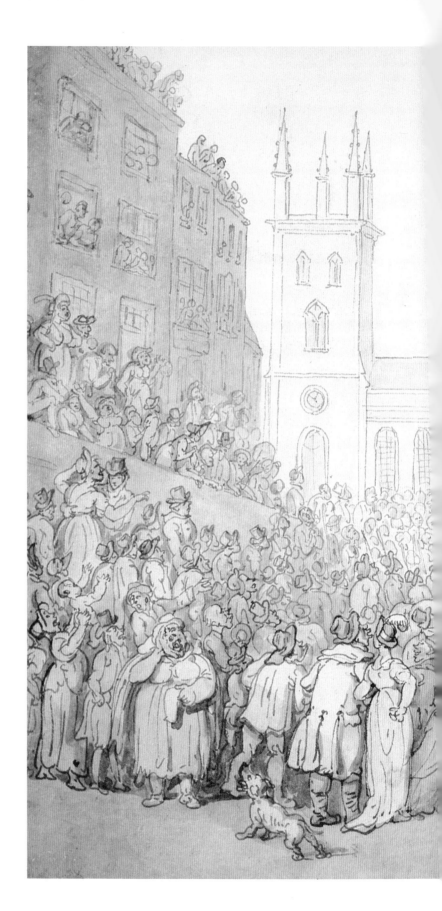

Execution at Newgate, London

THE HULKS

The cessation of transportation to America and the consequent swelling numbers of convicts in jail caused great embarrassment to the British government. As an emergency measure, an Act was passed in 1776 providing for transportees to be kept in hulks, old transport or naval vessels, while awaiting the anticipated renewal of transportation to America.

Hundreds of convicts were housed in hulks floating on the Thames near London, and at Plymouth and Portsmouth. Those who could not be crammed into the hulks had to remain in prisons, causing outrage amongst jail administrators all over the country. One estimate states that the prison population increased by 73% in the decade after 1776.

Riots broke out in these overcrowded conditions, escape attempts were rife, and disease spread rapidly through the convict inhabitants of many jails and hulks. Throughout the late 1770s and early 1780s, the government was besieged with pleas to do something to relieve the situation.

RENEWAL OF TRANSPORTATION

In 1779 and 1784, the government passed two further Acts concerning transportation, permitting the Crown to nominate places other than America to which convicts could be sent.

A Committee of Inquiry into Transportation was established in 1779 to investigate alternative destinations for transportees. The idea of setting up a self-sufficient penal colony was first mooted at this time, a departure from the traditional method of selling convict labour in established colonies. Joseph Banks suggested to this Committee that Botany Bay was the ideal place, but other alternatives were preferred. Africa, Gibraltar, Canada, Nova Scotia, West Indies, East Indies, New Zealand and the Falkland Islands were all considered as potential sites over the next few years.

By 1784 the British government had reluctantly concluded that it would not be possible to resume transportation to any existing British colonies. Local sentiment against the practice was running too high. As an alternative, the government approached the Portuguese to ask if British convicts might be of use in Portuguese colonies; the offer was declined. Slowly, reluctantly, the government turned to the costly alternative of a self-sufficient penal colony in an unsettled land.

Towards the end of 1784 the west coast of Africa seemed to be the most favoured site. On 29 December, Evan Nepean, Under Secretary of State, wrote:

It is at last determined that they [the convicts] shall forthwith be removed...to the coast of Africa...which you know in the routine of Punishment is considered as next in degree to that of Death.

It was hoped that the first batch of convicts could be established there by mid 1785. However, one delay after another forced the suspension of this plan until after the winter. In the meantime, under attack for the secrecy in which it had made those plans, the government convened another Committee to inquire into revisions of the Transportation Acts and into potential transportation destinations.

Witnesses to this Committee consistently condemned the African proposal and Secretary of State, Lord Sydney, ruefully recorded:

...from the mistaken humanity of some and the affected tenderness of others, every Plan, which the King's servants have proposed for transporting the convicts out of the Kingdom, has met with such opposition, that it has been almost impossible to carry any of them into Execution.

Once again, Botany Bay was suggested and Joseph Banks gave evidence as to the suitability of this location:

I have no doubt that the Soil of many Parts of the Eastern Coast of New South Wales between the Lattitudes of 30 & 40 is sufficiently fertile to support a Considerable Number of Europeans...Botany Bay is the only part of that Country which I have actually visited and I am confident that is in every respect adapted to the purpose...There are very few Inhabitants... they did not appear at all to be feared...there were some very large Trees and every where vast Quantities of Grass...From the Fertility of the Soil the timid Disposition of the Inhabitants and the climate being so analogous to that of Europe I give this place the preference to all that I have seen.

However, Botany Bay was to be overshadowed by its likely cost and by a newly proposed suggestion. In mid 1785 the Committee recommended that, subject to a favourable survey, the penal colony be established in Das Voltas Bay in Namibia (South West Africa), a location close to major trading routes and within three months sailing distance of England. A Navy vessel was dispatched to undertake the survey, returning in July 1786 with the news that the site was totally unsuitable. The last alternative within a comparatively short distance of England had been rejected.

BOTANY BAY

In desperation, the British government seized upon the only possibility left, one that had always sounded encouraging but had been bypassed because of the expense and distance involved–Botany Bay. On 18 August 1786 Lord Sydney wrote to the Lords Commissioners of the Treasury:

The several Goals [sic] and Places for the confinement of Felons in this Kingdom being in so crowded a State that the greatest danger is to be apprehended not only from their Escape but from Infectious Distempers which may hourly be expected to break out amongst them; His Majesty desirous of preventing by every possible means the ill consequences which might happen from either of these causes, has been pleased to signify to me His Royal Commands that Measures should immediately be pursued for sending out of this Kingdom such of the Convicts as are under sentence or order of Transportation...His Majesty has thought it advisable to fix upon Botany Bay, situated on the Coast of New South Wales...I am therefore commanded to signify to your Lordships His Majesty's pleasure that you do forthwith take such measures as may be necessary for providing a proper number of vessels for the conveyance of 750 Convicts to Botany Bay, together with such Provisions, Necessaries and Implements for agriculture as may be requisite for their Use after their arrival.

Signing the United States' Declaration of Independence

Prison hulk in Portsmouth harbour

Trial in progress at the Old Bailey

Enclosed with this letter, and with a similar letter to the Admiralty, was a document which has become known as the *Heads of a Plan*. It outlined the necessary preparations for the voyage and the estimated budget.

Heads of a Plan for effectually disposing of Convicts, and rendering their Transportation reciprocally beneficial both to themselves and to the State, by the Establishment of a Colony in New South Wales, a Country which, by the fertility and Salubrity of the Climate, connected with the remoteness of its situation (from whence it is hardly possible for Persons to return without permission), seems peculiarly adapted to answer the views of Government with respect to the providing a remedy for the Evils likely to result by the late alarming and numerous increase of Felons in this Country, and more particularly in the Metropolis...

That Government should immediately provide a certain number of Ships of a proper burthen to receive on board at least seven or eight hundred Convicts, and that one of them should be properly fitted for the accommodation of the Women to prevent their intercourse with the Men.

That these Ships should take on board as much Provisions as they can possibly stow, or at least a sufficient Quantity for two years consumption, supposing one year to be issued at whole allowance, and the other year's Provisions at half allowance, which will last two years longer, by which time it is presumed the Colony, with the Live Stock and Grain, which may be raised by a common Industry on the part of the New Settlers, will be fully sufficient for their maintenance and support....

The whole regulation and management of the Settlement should be committed to the Care of a discreet officer, and Provision should be made in all cases both Civil and Military by special Instructions under the Great Seal or otherwise, as may be thought proper.

This document also touched upon other potential benefits of the colony, apart from relieving the convict situation:

It may not be amiss to remark in favour of this Plan that considerable advantage will arise from the Cultivation of the New Zealand Hemp or Flax Plant in the new intended Settlement, the supply of which would be of great consequence to us as a Naval Power. As our Manufacturers are of opinion that Canvas made of it would be superior in strength and beauty to any Canvas made from the European Material, and that a Cable of the Circumference of ten Inches made from the former would be superior in strength to one of eighteen Inches made of the latter. The Threads or Filaments of this New Zealand Plant, are formed by nature with the most exquisite delicacy, and may be so minutely divided as to be manufactured into the finest Linens.

Most of the asiatic Productions may also without doubt be cultivated in the New Settlement, and in a few years may render our recourse to our European Neighbours for those Productions unnecessary.

It may also be proper to attend to the possibility of procuring from New Zealand any Quantity of Masts and Ship Timber for the use of our Fleets in India, as the distance between the two Countries is not greater than between Great Britain and America. It grows close to the Water's Edge, is of size and quality superior to any hitherto known, and may be obtained without difficulty.

The 'real' reason for the British government's decision to establish a colony at Botany Bay has been a cause for controversy amongst historians almost since the day the decision was announced. Some historians claim that the government's main concern was to establish a strategic base close to the trading routes to the Far East and that the convict problem was used as a cover for this ulterior motive. Others assert that new sources of supply were the main aim, that it was hoped that the timber and flax on Norfolk Island would provide the Royal Navy with masts and ropes for many years to come. Still others maintain that the government's only intention was to get rid of some convicts, regardless of the cost, to save its political face.

It seems most probable that, although the convict problem was the motivating force, the British government was not blind to the other potential benefits of this new settlement–its strategic location on the edge of the Pacific and its resources of land and raw materials.

'A DISCREET OFFICER'

The *Heads of a Plan* required that the 'regulation and management of the Settlement should be committed to the Care of a discreet officer'. By early September 1786 Captain Arthur Phillip of the Royal Navy had been selected to be that officer. His first commission required him to sail in December but this was patently impossible. The convoy of eleven ships that was to become known as the First Fleet eventually set sail in May 1787.

Captain John Hunter, also of the Royal Navy, was appointed second-in-command at sea, and given a dormant commission to succeed Phillip as Commander of the fleet and Governor of the colony should Phillip die or be incapable of performing his duties.

So, in the hands of these two men, Phillip and Hunter, lay the immediate futures of 750 convicts, the marines and sailors of the First Fleet and even the Aboriginal inhabitants of Botany Bay. The story of the voyage of the First Fleet will be told in the next stamp heritage book.

William Pitt, the British Prime Minister

Sydney's letter to the Treasury

Prisoners in a London street

George III

George III succeeded to the British throne in 1760 at the age of twenty-two, upon the death of his grandfather, George II. His reign lasted for sixty years, although from 1788 onwards he suffered periodic bouts of insanity. By 1811 he had become permanently insane and his son, later to become George IV, served as regent until George III's death.

This period was one of the most eventful and progressive in British history. George III's reign saw huge advances in the natural and physical sciences, a revolution in industry and manufacturing technology, a swing of population from the country to the cities, a burgeoning trade empire, improved literacy and national transport, abolition of the slave trade, administrative and fiscal reforms in government, war with France and America, Napoleon and Waterloo, as well as the discovery and settlement of eastern Australia.

George III himself was reputed to be obstinate, rash and tyrannical, and he has been blamed for causing the American War of Independence through his political ineptitude. However, it was he who approved the funds necessary for Cook's first voyage to the Pacific, when eastern Australia was discovered, and Banks, Solander and Cook were all presented to him upon their return, though at different times. On 17 August 1770 Cook recorded:

...I had the Honour of a hours Conference with the King the other day who was pleased to express his Approbation of my Conduct in Terms that were extremely pleasing to me...

It was also under George III's authority that the decision was made to found a penal settlement in New South Wales, a settlement which was well established by the time he died in 1820.

The 'George III' stamp features a portrait in oils from the studio of A. Ramsay, c.1767, held in the National Portrait Gallery, London, together with his signature from a manuscript in the National Library of Australia. In the background is a coloured rendition of a portion of an eighteenth century engraving, in the collection of the Guildhall Library, London, showing a line of convicts in chains.

George III

Political cartoon lampooning the King's abilities

32

Lord Sydney

In 1783, under the auspices of King George III, William Pitt (the Younger) became Prime Minister. In that same year, Mr Thomas Townshend (1733-1800) was raised to the peerage. As Lord Sydney, Townshend was Secretary of State in the Home Office from 1783 to 1789, the vital years during which the decision to establish a penal colony in New South Wales was made and executed.

It was Lord Sydney who bore responsibility for finding a solution to the convict problem and who, once that solution was determined, had to ensure that the plan was carried out. It was he who advised the Treasury and the Admiralty of the decision to send convicts to Botany Bay and who subsequently administered the preparations for the First Fleet and the affairs of the colony during its first months. The *Heads of a Plan* was prepared and distributed by his office.

Much of the delay between the onset of the convict problem and the determination of a solution has been attributed to Sydney. Nevertheless, he acquired the distinction of having his name bestowed by Arthur Phillip upon the first European settlement in Australia.

Convicts ready for transportation

The 'Lord Sydney' stamp features a portrait attributed to Gilbert Stuart, held by the Dixson Galleries, State Library of New South Wales, together with his signature. Again, as a reminder of the basic reason for the decision to settle Botany Bay, a line of chained convicts appears in the background, from an engraving held in the Guildhall Library, London.

Lord Sydney

33

Arthur Phillip

Arthur Phillip joined the Royal Navy in 1755 at the age of seventeen, after two years in the merchant marine. He served in the Mediterranean and the West Indies until 1763, when he was retired on half-pay with the rank of Lieutenant. For the next ten years, he concentrated on managing a farming property in Hampshire, before joining the Portuguese navy in 1774 to serve in the war between Portugal and Spain. During his four years in the Portuguese navy, he gained experience in the transportation of convicts by sea and was promoted to Captain.

In 1778 he returned to the Royal Navy, serving in India before again retiring on half-pay in 1784 after the American War of Independence. He was recalled to duty in 1786, when he was forty-eight years old, to be appointed as Captain General of the First Fleet and Governor-in-Chief of the penal colony to be established in New South Wales.

It is generally accepted that Phillip was chosen for the post because of his reputation as a competent, trustworthy officer and an excellent administrator. He was also available at the right time and had previous experience in both the transportation of convicts and in farming and land management, all essential qualities for the Governor of this new colony.

Phillip proved to be an excellent choice for the position and served as Governor of New South Wales until December 1792, when illness forced him to return to Britain. He continued to serve in the Royal Navy until 1805 and attained the rank of Admiral before his death nine years later.

The portrait of Arthur Phillip reproduced on the stamp was painted by F. Wheatley in 1786, and is now in the National Portrait Gallery, London. His signature is reproduced from a document in the Mitchell Library, State Library of New South Wales.

Arthur Phillip

John Hunter

Captain John Hunter was selected as Phillip's second-in-command at sea and also held a dormant commission to succeed as Governor should Phillip die or be incapacitated. A protégé of Howe, the First Lord of the Admiralty, Hunter had initially been considered as an alternative to Phillip for the command of the First Fleet.

A year older than Phillip, Hunter had joined the Royal Navy in 1754 and had served in North America and the West Indies. Promoted to Captain in 1782, he had a reputation as a gentle, reserved, humane and competent master and a skilled navigator and map-maker.

Hunter returned to Britain in 1792, but was sent back to New South Wales upon the enforced resignation of Arthur Phillip, and served as Governor there from 1795 until 1800. He died in 1821, having reached the rank of Vice-Admiral in the service of the Royal Navy.

Hunter's portrait was painted in 1815 by W. M. Bennett and is now held in the Dixson Galleries, State Library of New South Wales. His signature is reproduced from a document in the Mitchell Library, State Library of New South Wales. In the background to this stamp are depicted some of the Aboriginal inhabitants of New South Wales ranged along the shore. Based on a painting by William Bradley in the Mitchell Library, this image serves to remind us that there were others more tragically affected by the British decision to settle Australia than the convicts, marines and sailors aboard the First Fleet.

John Hunter

Aborigines on the shore, by Bradley

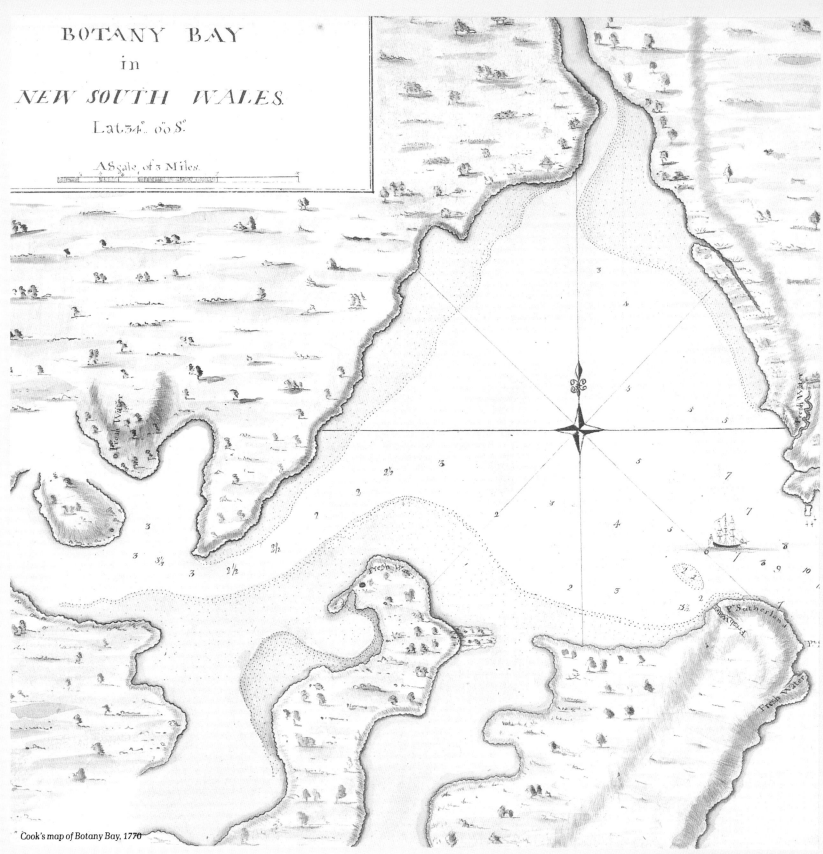

BOTANY BAY
in
NEW SOUTH WALES.
Lat.34°. 00 S°.

A Scale of 3 Miles.

Cook's map of Botany Bay, 1770

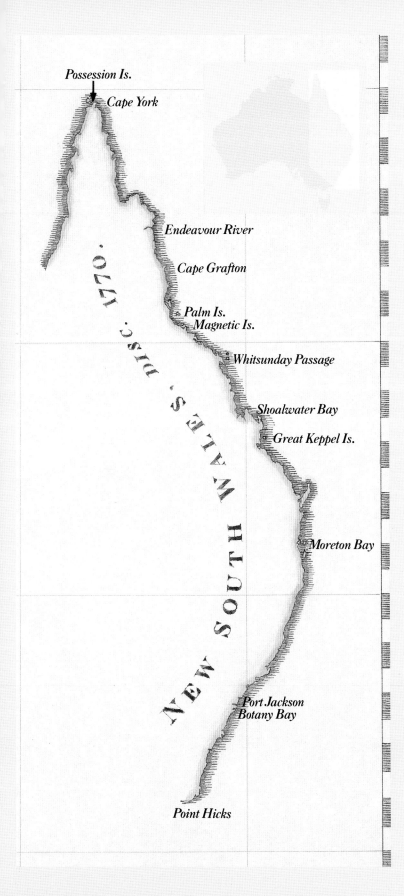

Possession Is.

Cape York

Endeavour River

Cape Grafton

Palm Is.
Magnetic Is.

Whitsunday Passage

Shoalwater Bay

Great Keppel Is.

Moreton Bay

Port Jackson
Botany Bay

Point Hicks

NEW SOUTH WALES DISC. 1770.

BIBLIOGRAPHY

General

Clark, C. M. H. *A History of Australia*. Melbourne, Melbourne University Press, 1962. Volume I.

King, J. *'In the Beginning...'–The Story of the Creation of Australia From the Original Writings*. Melbourne, Macmillan, 1985.

Plumb, J. H. *England in the Eighteenth Century*. Harmondsworth, Penguin, 1950, 1983.

New Holland: Cook's Voyage

Beaglehole, J. C. *The Life of Captain James Cook*. London, A. & C. Black, 1974.

Beaglehole, J. C. (Ed.). *The Endeavour Journal of Joseph Banks, 1768-1771*. Sydney, The Trustees of the Public Library of New South Wales in association with Angus & Robertson, 1962. 2 volumes.

Carr, D. J. (Ed.). *Sydney Parkinson–Artist of Cook's Endeavour Voyage*. Canberra, British Museum (Natural History) in association with Australian National University Press, 1983.

Diment, J. A., Humphries, C. J., Newington, L. & Shaughnessy, E. *Catalogue of the Natural History Drawings Commissioned by Joseph Banks on the Endeavour Voyage 1768-1771 Held in the British Museum (Natural History). Part I: Botany: Australia*. London, Meckler Publishing in association with the British Museum (Natural History), 1984.

Parkinson, S. *A Journal of a Voyage to the South Seas, In his Majesty's Ship The Endeavour*. London, Stanfield Parkinson, 1773.

Price, A. G. (Ed.). *The Explorations of Captain James Cook in the Pacific as told by Selections of his own Journals 1768-1779*. Sydney, Angus & Robertson, 1969.

Villiers, A. *Captain Cook, the Seamen's Seaman*. Harmondsworth, Penguin, 1969.

New South Wales: The Decision To Settle

Blainey, G. *The Tyranny of Distance–How Distance Shaped Australia's History*. Melbourne, Sun Books, 1966, 1983.

Frost, A. *Convicts and Empire–A Naval Question 1776-1811*. Melbourne, Oxford University Press, 1980.

Mackay, D. *A Place of Exile–The European Settlement of New South Wales*. Melbourne, Oxford University Press, 1985.

Martin, G. (Ed.). *The Founding of Australia–The Argument about Australia's Origins*, Sydney, Hale & Ironmonger, 1978.

Plumb, J. H. *The First Four Georges*. Glasgow, Fontana/Collins, 1966.

Robson, L. L. *The Convict Settlers of Australia*. Melbourne, Melbourne University Press, 1965.

Shaw, A. G. L. *Convicts and the Colonies*. London, Faber & Faber, 1966.

ACKNOWLEDGEMENTS

Australia Post wishes to thank the staff of all the source institutions listed below for their co-operation and assistance. Thanks are also due to Dr. L. L. Robson, Reader in History, University of Melbourne, for his assistance during preparation of the text. Photographs and drawings have been reproduced with kind permission from the following sources:

Alecto Historical Editions, London: p. 21 Botany store at British Museum (Natural History); p. 23 Alecto's printing press.

Bridgeman Art Library, London: p. 27 Trial in Progress at the Old Bailey, Thomas Rowlandson (from original in Guildhall Library, London).

British Library, London: p. 38 James Cook's Map of Botany Bay, 1770.

British Museum (Natural History), London: p. 3, 16-23 Banks' *Florilegium*–sketches by Sydney Parkinson and watercolour illustrations; p. 9 Sketch of kangaroo by Sydney Parkinson; p. 14-15 Self-portrait of Sydney Parkinson.

Cranbrook School, Sydney: p. 9 The naturalists discover a kangaroo & p. 12-13 Banks conferring with Solander, both from 'Captain Cook' stained glass window by John Lamb Lyon, late nineteenth century.

Dixson Galleries, State Library of New South Wales: p. 32-33 Portrait of Lord Sydney, attributed to Gilbert Stuart; p. 36-37 Portrait of John Hunter, W. M. Bennett, 1815.

Guildhall Library, London: p. 27 Prison-Ship in Portsmouth harbour, Convicts going on board, in E. W. Cooke, *Shipping and Craft,* London, 1829, plate 27; p. 29 Prisoners stopping at the Baptist's Head in St. John's Lane & p. 30, 32-33 Representation of the Transports going from Newgate to take water at Blackfriars, both in *The Malefactor's Register; or the Newgate and Tyburn Calendar, etc.* London, Alexander Hogg, c.1779.

Jutta Hösel/Australasian Nature Transparencies: p. 40 *Banksia serrata.*

Mitchell Library, State Library of New South Wales: p. 34-35 Signature of Arthur Phillip; p. 36-37 Signature of John Hunter, First interview with the native women at Port Jackson, William Bradley, 1788.

Museum of London: p. 24-25 Execution at Newgate, Thomas Rowlandson; p. 31 Political Cartoon for the Year 1775.

National Art Gallery of New Zealand, Wellington: p. 7 Portrait of Captain James Cook, John Webber.

National Library of Australia: p. 12-13 Signature of Joseph Banks; p. 30-31 Signature of George III.

National Maritime Museum, London: p. 7 Admiralty plan of His Majesty's Bark *Endeavour* as fitted at Deptford in 1768.

National Portrait Gallery, London: p. 4-5 William Pitt addressing the House of Commons, K. A. Hickel, 1793; p. 27 Signing the United States' Declaration of Independence; p. 29 Portrait of William Pitt, John Hoppner, 1805; p. 30-31 Portrait of George III, Studio of A. Ramsay, c. 1767; p. 34-35 Portrait of Arthur Phillip, F. Wheatley, 1786; cover & p. 12-13 Portrait of Joseph Banks, Sir Joshua Reynolds (formerly held by Parham Park, England).

Public Record Office, London: p. 2 Heads of a Plan, 18 August 1786; p. 29 Letter from Lord Sydney to Lords Commissioners of the Treasury, 18 August 1786.

The World of Interiors magazine, London: p. 19 Cleaning a *Florilegium* copperplate at Alecto; p. 21 Inking a *Florilegium* copperplate at Alecto.

University of Melbourne (Baillieu Library): p. 10-11 The *Endeavour* beached at the Endeavour River, in J. Hawkesworth (Ed.), *An Account of the Voyages Undertaken by the Order of His Present Majesty etc.* London, W. Strahan & T. Cadell, 1773, plate 19.

University of Melbourne (The Grimwade Collection): p. 9 Two of the Natives of New Holland Advancing to Combat & p. 15 Sydney Parkinson at his desk, both in S. Parkinson, *A Journal of a Voyage to the South Seas, in His Majesty's Ship, the Endeavour, etc.* London, Stanfield Parkinson, 1773, frontispiece & plate 27.